Ave, Maria!
Praying the Rosary

Robert B. Kelly

First published in 1997 by
KEVIN MAYHEW LTD
Rattlesden
Bury St Edmunds
Suffolk IP30 0SZ

0 1 2 3 4 5 6 7 8 9

ISBN 1 84003 052 6
Catalogue No 1500124

Front cover: Paper Collages by Bettina Healey
Cover design by Jaquetta Sergeant
Typesetting by Louise Hill
Printed and bound in Great Britain

Contents

INTRODUCTION

This book offers four aids towards praying the rosary, based on the fundamental principles that the rosary:

- is meant to offer a simple pattern of organised, regular prayer;
- is a prolonged meditation on the mysteries of our salvation as won through the life, death, resurrection and glorification of Christ;
- is based on a cycle of 150 prayers, in imitation of the 150 psalms of the psalter.

The four key ideas are:

1. To offer a pattern of regular prayer, where each decade is focused on one of the 'mysteries' of our salvation. This means that the real Rosary is Christo-centric, based and centred on Christ, sent by the Father, in the Spirit, who is the sole mediator between humankind and God, the First-born from the dead through whom all others can achieve resurrection and live with God.

For this reason, each of the mysteries is accompanied by at least one, often several references to passages from the Gospels, so that your prayer may have this proper focus: that it rise, through Christ, in the Spirit, to the Father.

Where there are several Gospel passages, you may prefer to follow the liturgical cycle, and concentrate on Matthew when we are in Year A, etc.

2. The whole point of these 'mysteries' is to speak to us of things which cannot be put into words. Sometimes the traditional titles for the 'mysteries' can block their meaningfulness, precisely because we are too familiar with them. Each time we confront one of these mysteries, we need to ask ourselves, what is God trying to say to me through this event? It may help to re-describe the event, in your own words. Instead of 'mystery', try the word 'sign' or 'symbol'.

With each of the mysteries, a prayer thought is proposed (usually based on prayers from the liturgies of the Church celebrating this mystery). But these are just to launch you on your way. Ideally, each time you confront a 'mystery' you should give it the chance to say something new to you, something you have never heard or thought of before. In this sense, though the mystery remains the same, its name can change every time you meet it.

3. Since a large part of the inspiration behind the 'invention' of the Rosary was to imitate the Psalter of 150 Psalms, each of the mysteries is also accompanied by a selection of appropriate psalm verses.

You may like to pray this psalm, as a single prayer, having reflected for a few moments on the Gospel presentation of the mystery.

Alternatively, you may like to divide the Psalm up into ten prayerful invocations, one to accompany each recitation of the 'Hail, Mary'.

4. Sometimes, in your personal praying of the 'Hail, Mary', you may find that you can use quotes from the Gospel passages or some of the smaller psalm portions like *clausulæ*, that is, you can interpret them as describing or honouring Christ, and add them in the middle of your recitation of the 'Hail, Mary'.

For example:

THIRD JOYFUL MYSTERY

THE PRESENTATION IN THE TEMPLE

'Hail Mary, full of grace.
The Lord is with thee.
Blessed art thou among women,
and blessed is the fruit of thy womb, Jesus . . .
. . . Jesus, the salvation God has prepared
in the presence of all peoples,
a light to give revelation to the Gentiles
and to give glory to God's people.'
Holy Mary, Mother of God . . .

THE JOYFUL MYSTERIES

1 THE ANNUNCIATION

Luke 1:26-38

'See, you will conceive and bear a son . . .'
'Let it be done to me according to your word.'

Christ our Lord came to save humanity,
    by becoming human himself.
The Virgin Mary,
    by responding to the angel's message in faith
    consented to bear God's Son,
    and by the power of the Holy Spirit
        she conceived.
'The maiden is with child,
    and soon she will give birth to a son,
    and she will call him Emmanuel, God-with-us.'
        (Isaiah 7:14b)
So the promise made to Israel came true;
    so the hope of all humankind was fulfilled
    beyond all human expectations.
Jesus came to the waiting world.
May the presence of Mary's child
    fill the void in our life.
May others find Christ in us.

Psalm 39

1 I waited, I waited for the Lord
   and he stooped down to me;
   he heard my cry.

2 Happy are those who trust in God;
   many shall see
   and come to have trust in the Lord.

3 O Lord my God, what wonders and signs
   you have worked for us!
   Who else is like you!

4 I shall proclaim your wonders,
   I shall sing of your signs;
   they are more than I can tell!

5 What is it you ask of us?
   Not sacrifice – but simply an open ear.
   So here I am Lord.

6 What you want is that I should do your will.
   My God, to do your will
   fills my heart with the greatest pleasure!

7 Lord, keep me in your compassion.
   Let your merciful love and your truth
   enfold me.

8 Some will be appalled,
   jeer at what happens to me.
   Theirs is the real shame.

9 But those who really seek you
   will rejoice and be glad;
   they will welcome your saving help.

10 As for me, poor as I am,
     the Lord thinks of me.
     He is my help, my rescue.

2 THE VISITATION

Luke 1:39-45

'The baby in my womb danced for joy!'

May we echo the song of thanksgiving of Elizabeth!
May our hearts dance with joy!
For thanks to Mary, the Lord is with us.
But Mary's loving welcome of the Lord's presence
     was no passive acceptance.
Mary goes to visit Elizabeth and assist her in her
     need.
May we be ever open to the Spirit
     so that in helping those we find around us,
     the presence of the Lord may be felt
     – in a way that makes people want to sing
        and dance!

Psalm 91

1 It is good to give thanks to the Lord,
   to make music to honour our God.

2 It is good to proclaim God's love in
       the morning,
   at night to sing of his wonderful truth.

3 For what the Lord does fills my heart with
       gladness,
   all that he does makes me want to dance
       with joy!

4 Lord, how great are the works of your hands
   Lord, how great the plans you have for us!

5 Only the foolish are blind to your greatness
   deaf to your music, and lame to your dance.

6 Those who are evil are weedy and feeble,
   just like the grass which sprouts and then dies.

7 Those who learn to live in your justice
   will flourish, grow taller than the tallest of trees.

8 With our roots firmly planted in the garden
       of God
   we shall flourish in the house of the Lord.

9 Though we are old, we are still green,
       the sap rises;
   we can still sing out the praises of God!

10 Proclaim the Lord's justice, his truth,
       his salvation;
    dance to his glory, sing praise to his name!

3 THE NATIVITY

Luke 2:6-14

*'A Saviour has been born for you,
the Christ, the Lord.'*

A birth:
   such a small step for such a new tiny person.
The birth of Christ:
   such a leap for humankind!
In the mystery of the incarnation
   God shows to the eyes of faith
   his eternal Word.
We share a glimpse in faith
   of God's glory, grace and truth.
In him we see made visible
   the God we cannot see;
   no one can see the glory of God,
   yet now that glory is one like us.
The Word,
   eternal, before all ages,
   condescends to be locked in our time.
Made lowly like us,
   he raises all to himself.
The 'God-said' through whom 'and-so-it-was',
   come to restore creation to its original unity.
God has become one with humankind

and humankind has become one again with God.
It is not one person's birthday we celebrate,
   but our own possibility of rebirth.
God grant that we may know the Word,
   hear the Word and live the life of the Word;
   see the Light and the live the life of the Light;
   know the Truth and live the life of the Truth;
   celebrate the Glory and come to live the life
      of Glory.

Psalms 95, 96, 97

1 Sing a new song to the Lord!
   Sing to the Lord, all the earth!
   Sing to the Lord, and bless his name!
2 Let your song last as long as the help that
      he gives,
   day upon day, and year upon year!
3 Proclaim to all nations his glory is here;
   tell all the peoples, salvation is here!
4 Let the heavens rejoice and the earth be glad,
   for the Lord has come, the Lord is here!
5 The Lord has come to rule the earth,
   to rule with truth and justice!
6 All peoples, see the glory of the Lord!
   The light has come for those who are just,
   joy has come for the upright of heart.
7 Sing a new song to the Lord!
   Sing in praise of the wonders he works!

Sing the salvation that falls from his hands!
8 The Lord has made known his salvation,
   has shown his justice to the nations.
   The truth and the love he promised is here!
9 All the ends of the earth have seen the salvation
    of the Lord.
   So shout to the Lord, all creation,
   ring out your joy!
10 The Lord has come to rule the earth,
   to rule with truth and justice!

4 THE PRESENTATION IN THE TEMPLE

Luke 2:22-40

'My eyes have seen your salvation . . .'

God fulfilled the hope of Simeon,
   who did not die until he had the opportunity
   to welcome the Messiah.
May we be prepared, like Simeon,
   to meet Christ,
   . . . wherever,
   . . . whenever.
May we recognise all the opportunities
   of encounters with Christ
   which are offered to us.

May the Spirit enlighten us
   to see the glory of God
   and the light of his salvation
   – even in those places we least expect it.

Psalm 26

1 The Lord is my light and my help,
    whom shall I fear?

2 The Lord is my strength,
    of whom shall I be afraid?

3 There is one thing I ask of the Lord,
    to dwell in his house.

4 If only I could live in the house of the Lord
    all the days of my life.

5 In the Lord's house I find safety
    and shelter from all evil.

6 Lord, hear my prayer,
    you know it is you that I seek.

7 Lord, do not hide from me,
    let me see your face.

8 Even if my family were to desert me,
    the Lord will never abandon me!

9 I know I shall the see Lord's goodness
    in the land of the living.

10 Hope in the Lord!
    Hold firm and take heart!
    Hope in the Lord!

5 THE FINDING OF THE CHILD JESUS IN THE TEMPLE

Luke 2:41-51

*'Do you not know that I must
be in my Father's house?'*

Where is my Father's house?
In becoming man,
   Jesus adopted our human family.
Through Jesus,
   we become the adopted sons and daughters
     of God.
The Father's house becomes our house.
In becoming man,
   Jesus accepted to dwell in time,
   to be obedient to the forces that govern
     human life.
In accepting our weakness,
   he gave immortal value to our mortal nature
May we, though prisoners of our own time,
   learn to live in obedience to that eternal life
   which our Father promises us.

Psalm 83

1 How magnificent
   is the Lord God's house!

2 How I long and yearn
   to be in my Father's house!
3 Then would I sing for joy
   to God, the living God!
4 Yet here in God's mighty house
   even the sparrow finds a home.
5 See the nest in the rafters,
   the fledgelings who live next to your altar!
6 Listen to their simple song of joy,
   happy to be alive!
7 Happy those who dwell in your house,
   singing your praise.
8 One day in your house
   is better than a thousand elsewhere.
9 Even to live on your doorstep
   is better than living among the wicked.
10 How I long and yearn
   to be in my Father's house!

THE SORROWFUL MYSTERIES

1 THE AGONY IN THE GARDEN OF GETHSEMANE

Matthew 26:36-46; Mark 14:32-42 Luke 22:39-46

'Watch and pray . . .'

What does God really want of me?
You asked yourself that question
   in the desert after you were baptised.
You saw then
   that you had to feed people
   – not with ordinary bread
   but with the Bread of the Word
   and the Bread of Life.
This night, at this Supper,
   in the breaking of the bread
   and the sharing of the cup,
   you did it.
You saw then
   that you had to rule people,
   not by lording it over people,
   but by being their servant.
This night, at this Supper,
   in washing your disciples' feet
   you did it.

You saw then
>   that you had to replace the old Temple,
>   that through you
>   would effective prayer pass to God;
>   prayer of praise and thanksgiving,
>   but also the prayer of sacrifice,
>   of life given, to the very end,
>   sweated to the last drop of blood.

This night, at this Supper,
>   you pledged it.
>   Is this really what God wants?

What a remarkable prayer,
>   that remains open-ended!

There is no spoken 'Amen' to real prayer.
>   It is how we live on the morrow,
>   the promise of prayer we say today,
>   that is our only true 'Amen'.
>   Lord, teach us to live 'Amen'.

Psalm 54

1   O God, listen to my pleas!
>   Do not be deaf to my prayer!
>   Listen, and give answer,
>   I am at my wit's end with worry.

2   My heart trembles within me,
>   I feel death's dark shadow is near.
>   See how I fear and I tremble
>   at the thought of the horrors that await me!

3 If only I had wings I would fly
   and find a place of rest.
   I would fly as far as I could
   to escape, and be at peace.
4 Here, in the city, where can we find peace?
   Nothing but violence and strife!
   Truth and deceit haunt the place,
   like muggers that haunt the night.
5 If it had been an enemy that had done it,
   that I might understand.
   If it were a rival that had risen against me,
   that would have been no surprise.
6 But you, a friend
   – and a close friend at that!
   You who walked and talked and shared with me
   – even stood at my side in the temple!
7 The traitor's tongue is softer than butter,
   his promises ooze out like oil.
   But his heart is hard
   and his words cut sharp.
8 So to the Lord I raise my cry
   – who else but God can help me now!
   What is left for me but to pour out *my* woes
   morning, noon and night.
9 Yet I know that the Lord will give me peace
   deliver me from those who attack me.
   No matter how many the enemies ranged
      against me,

the Lord hears my voice!
10 So cast off your cares on the Lord,
he will support you;
The Lord will see me through.
O Lord, I trust in you.

2 THE SCOURGING AT THE PILLAR

Matthew 27:15-26; Mark 15:6-20
Luke 23:13-25; John 18:29-19:1

'Whom do you want . . . Barabbas or Jesus?'

The scourging at the pillar
  – no more than a tiny mention in the Gospels,
  and yet it has captivated believers' attention
  in prayer, in painting, in sculpture.
Perhaps because it is the turning point.
We have just been offered a choice:
  do you want the Son of man?
  or do you want Bar-Abbas, the Son-of-the-Father?
And what do we want?
We shouted for the Son-of-the-Father,
  'Give us Barabbas!'
This Jesus is all too human,
  and as if to prove it for ourselves,
  we want to see the colour of his blood.

See,
> when we scourge him,
> does he not bleed like the rest of us?

Instead of choosing
> the one who sheds his own blood,
> we chose one who shed others' blood.

Canticle (Isaiah 53:1-6)

1 Who has believed what we have heard?
> To whom has God's power been revealed?

2 He grew up like a young plant in front of us,
> like a fresh sapling rises from the arid ground.

3 No beauty, no majesty,
> nothing to make us want to look at him.

4 Despised and rejected by men,
> a man of sorrows, no stranger to suffering.

5 A man of sorrows from whom people hid
> their faces,
> we despised him and thought he was worthless.

6 Yet ours were those sufferings he bore;
> the sorrows he carried were ours.

7 We thought God wanted him punished,
> we thought he should be struck down.

8 Yet ours were the faults for which he was
> wounded,
> crushed and brought low for our sins.

9 On him was laid the punishment that makes
> us whole,

and by his wounds we are healed.
10 When we had wandered like sheep,
    he became the lamb that takes sins away.

3 THE CROWNING WITH THORNS

Matthew 27:27-30

'Hail, King of the Jews!'

John 18:33-19:9

'You are a king, then?'

So you are a king!
But look at the crimson trophy,
    a crown made of thorns.
Poor bush,
    cut,
    twisted,
    used for a purpose
    that nature never intended.
Yet this is the bush
    that catches the ram by the horns
    and so redeems Isaac.
This is the bush
    that burns
    without ever being consumed.

This is our King,
    cut down,
    twisted,
    turned to a purpose he never intended.
This is our King
    who catches Satan by the horns
    and so redeems all humanity.
This is our King,
    utterly burnt out,
    whose dominion can never end.

Psalm 71

1 O God, give your justice to the king
    that he may judge your people in justice
    and your poor in right judgement.

2 Like the rivers that flow down from the hills,
    may peace come tumbling from his hands,
    and justice like mountain-streams.

3 May he defend the poor of the people;
    may he save the children of the needy;
    may he crush those who oppress the poor.

4 May he live for ever, like the sun and
     the moon.
    May his reign give life to all creation,
    bring justice and peace to all.

5 May his enemies fall before him.
    May kings be his servants.
    May all nations serve him.

6 For he hears the cry of the poor and the needy,
   he rescues all who are helpless,
   he shows pity on those who are poor.

7 He saves the weak and downtrodden.
   He delivers the poor from oppression.
   To him, every drop of their blood is precious.

8 May he give food in plenty to his people,
   may his people flourish and thrive.
   Then shall all the world bless him.

9 May his name be blessed for ever,
   may all nations bless his name,
   may all be blessed in him.

10 Blessed be the Lord our God,
   ever blessed his glorious name.
   May his glory fill the earth.

4 Jesus Carries His Cross

Matthew 27:31-44; Mark 15:2-32
Luke 23:26-43

'They led him away to crucify him.'

The cross.
Mass-produced in silver and gold
   and worn with ease,
   with never a thought.
Is that how we carry the cross today?
In carrying the cross,
   Jesus was bearing our faults
   – but bearing them once and for all
   so that we might die to our faults
   and live for holiness.
By his wounds we have been healed.

Canticle (Isaiah 53:6-12)

1 When we had wandered like sheep,
   he became the lamb that takes sins away.

2 He bore all his affliction humbly,
   he never once opened his mouth.

3 Like the silence of the lamb led to the
    slaughter,
   like the sheep that is dumb before its
    shearers.

4 Seized by force, judged by law
   was there no one to plead in his favour?
5 Torn from the land of the living
   stricken with the guilt of the people.
6 They gave him a grave with the wicked,
   with the rich a tomb.
7 Yet he had done no harm,
   no lie had ever passed his lips.
8 Crushed with suffering,
   to do the Lord's will.
9 By offering his life in atonement,
   he wins life for himself and his heirs.
10 In letting himself be counted as a sinner,
   he carried the sins of all in intercession.

5 JESUS DIES ON THE CROSS

John 19:26-34

*'. . . pierced his side and at once
there came out blood and water.'*

As Adam, the first bridegroom, slept,
   God drew Eve out of his side.
As Christ, the new and eternal Bridegroom,
   slept the sleep of death on the cross
   God drew the Church, the new Eve,
   out of his pierced side.

By the wood of the tree,
  Adam and Eve proved their disobedience.
By the wood of the tree,
  the new Adam proved his utter obedience.
As the children of Adam and Eve inherited death,
    so the children of the new Adam and the
      new Eve
    shall inherit eternal life.
May we,
    who bear the human likeness of Adam
      and Eve,
    put on the likeness of Christ our Lord
    and pass with him through death to life.

Psalm 30

1 You alone, O Lord, are my refuge;
   let me never be put to shame.
   In your justice, set me free,
   hear me and come quickly to rescue me.
2 Be the rock on which I find shelter,
   the stronghold that offers me safety.
   You are my rock! You are my stronghold!
   Lead me, guide me, O Lord.
3 Keep me from the traps they have set for me,
   for you are my defender, O Lord.
   Into your hands I commend my spirit.
   You are the Lord who will redeem me.

4 Lord, have mercy,
  you know my distress.
  Eyes raw with crying,
  no voice left, no heart.

5 My days are full of sorrow,
  my years are full of sighs.
  Suffering has shattered my strength,
  my bones feel like jelly.

6 My enemies have got the better of me,
  their scorn has won the day.
  Even my friends are afraid to be seen with me.

7 Passers-by avoid me in the street.
  I smell fear all around,
  these people plotting against me,
  working for my downfall.

8 Yet still I trust in the Lord,
  and call to him alone for help:
  'I place my life in your hands,
  save me from my enemies.'

9 I trust in your love to save me,
  I long to see your face.
  Let those who mock my trust in you
  be the ones who suffer true shame.

10 I am sure you will hear my pleas,
   will listen to my cries for help.
   All you who hope in the Lord,
   be strong and courageous of heart.

THE GLORIOUS MYSTERIES

1 THE RESURRECTION

Matthew 28:1-10; Mark 16:1-7
Luke 24:1-7

'Do not be afraid! He has risen!'

Luke 24:13-35

*'. . . and they recognised him
in the breaking of the bread.'*

By raising Christ
    God has conquered death's power over us,
    opening up for us the way to eternal life.
May our eyes be always open
    to the joy of the Easter morning,
    and never clouded in doubt.
May Christ walk with us,
    even though we may not always
    recognise him immediately.
May the risen Lord breathe on our minds,
    open our eyes,
    set our hearts on fire,
    that we may know him in the breaking of
        the bread
    and follow him in his risen life.

Psalm 117

1 Give thanks to the Lord, for he is good,
    for his love is unending.
  Let all the people of God sing his praises,
    for his love is unending.

2 When I was in distress I called to the Lord,
    and he rescued me.
  With the Lord at my side, who should I fear?
    Who can do anything against me?

3 When they thought I was defeated and
    thrust down,
    the Lord was my Saviour.
  The Lord is my strength and my song
    the Lord is my Saviour.

4 It is the Lord who has triumphed,
    for the Lord raised me up.
  I shall not die, but I shall live,
    and sing for ever of what he has done.

5 They thought that I was punished,
    that I was doomed to die.
  Instead God opened up to me the gate of Life,
    where only the just may enter.

6 I pour out my praise to the Lord,
    for he listened and gave me answer.
  I give thanks to the Lord my God,
    for he is my Saviour

7 The stone which the builders rejected
    has become the corner-stone!

Such is the work of the Lord,
 let all who see it, marvel and give praise!
8 This is the day that the Lord has made;
 let us rejoice and be glad.
The day of triumph and salvation;
 let us rejoice and be glad.
9 Blessed for ever is the one
 who comes in the name of the Lord.
Blessed for ever is the one
 who leads us to the house of the Lord.
10 You are our God, we thank and praise you,
 for your love is unending.
Give thanks to the Lord for he is good,
 for his love is unending.

2 THE ASCENSION

Matthew 28:16-20; Mark 16:14-19
Acts 1:1-11

'You are my witnesses ... go, baptise all nations ...'

If Christ is our mediator,
 why did he leave us?
Why has he passed beyond our sight?
Christ has gone,
 not without us,
 but before us.

Christ is gone ahead,
   as our hope;
   where he has gone,
   we hope to follow.
He goes ahead
   to claim not only his share of eternal glory
   but to stake our claim to ours.
By taking Christ out of sight,
   God leads us to seek him in others,
   to bring others to see him in us:
   'Why stand looking into heaven?'
May the Holy Spirit clothe us with power,
   give us the strength
   to bring the Good News to others,
   to be Good News to others.

Psalm 46

1 Clap your hands together, all you peoples,
   sing out to God with shouts of joy!
2 For the Lord is the King of all the earth
   he is the Mighty One, Lord of all.
3 See how he puts all peoples under us,
   send us out to master the nations.
4 Like riches that a son inherits from his father
   is the glory that our God gives to us.
5 God goes up, acclaimed with shouts of joy;
   the trumpets sound as the Lord goes up.
6 Sing praises to our God, sing praises;

praise him as the King, sing his praises!

7 God is the King of all the earth
  Sing his praise as best you can!

8 God is the King over all nations,
  his throne is over all peoples.

9 Gathered round the throne are all peoples,
  Jews or Gentiles, all bow to him.

10 The Lord is God who rules over all,
   he alone is King of all.

3 THE COMING OF THE HOLY SPIRIT

Acts 2:1-11

'They were all filled with the Holy Spirit . . .'

We have been waiting since our Easter,
    since our passover with Christ in our baptism.
Fifty days?
Feels more like fifty years!
Lord, see your people gathered here in prayer,
    open to receive your Spirit's flame.
May it come to rest in our hearts
    casting out all division of word and tongue
    so that with one voice and with one tongue
    we shall sing our dreams and our visions!

Psalm 103

1 Bless the Lord, my soul,
   and say how great is our God.

2 Majesty, glory and light
   are like robes that speak of his might.

3 Like we might put up a tent
   you created the world.

4 You walk on the wings of the wind,
   wind and fire are at your command.

5 Who can count the wonders of the Lord,
   all that he created in wisdom?

6 The universe is full of your riches,
   all life is the gift of your hand.

7 All that lives looks to you
   for their daily bread.

8 You give, we harvest;
   what falls from your hands feeds us all.

9 But if you hold back your spirit,
   we fall back into dust.

10 When you send forth your spirit,
    new life is born from your breath.

4 THE ASSUMPTION OF MARY INTO HEAVEN

Luke 1:46-55

'The Mighty One has raised up the lowly!'

Just as all die in Adam,
    so all will be brought to life in Christ.
But each of us in our proper order:
    first, Christ himself,
    the first-born from the dead;
    then, those who belong to him.
Mary
    – as the one who gave birth to Christ,
    the Son of God, the Lord of life,
    – how could God allow decay to touch her body?
She brought forth the innocent lamb
    who takes away our sins.
In choosing her from among all women
    to be the mother of your Son
    you made her our advocate with you.
In her assumption
    we see the beginning and the model of the
        Church,
    a sign of comfort and of hope to a pilgrim
        people,
    called to that same perfection which she
        already enjoys.

Listen, Lord, to her prayers
  on our behalf.

Canticle (Luke 1:46-55)

1 My soul magnifies the Lord,
    and my spirit rejoices in God my Saviour.

2 He has looked upon the lowliness of his
      handmaid.

3 Yes, from now and for ever,
    all generations shall call me blessed;
    for the Mighty One has done great things
      for me.

4 Holy is his name!

5 His mercy is from age to age
    toward those who fear him.

6 He has shown the strength of his arm,
    he has scattered the proud in their arrogance
      of heart.

7 He has tumbled the mighty from their thrones
    and has raised up the lowly.

8 He has filled the hungry with good things,
    sent the rich away empty.

9 He has come in his mercy to the help of
      Israel, his servant,
    just as he promised to our ancestors,
    to Abraham and to his descendants for ever.

10 My soul magnifies the Lord,
     and my spirit rejoices in God my Saviour.

5 THE GLORY OF MARY AND OF ALL THE SAINTS IN HEAVEN

Luke 1:26-38

'Hail, full of grace!'

Praise to you, holy Queen,
    Mother of mercy!
To you who are the source of
    our life, its sweetness and its hope, praise!
We, the children of Eve,
    banished from Paradise,
    cry to you for help.
From this valley of tears,
    we raise our laments and our pleas to you.
We pray you to be our advocate before God,
    and to turn towards us, your eyes full of mercy.
And when our exile is over,
    bring us to your Son, Jesus.
To you,
    most merciful,
    most loving,
    most gentle, Virgin
    we pray
    that we too may be found worthy of the promise
    which Christ has won for us.

Psalm 44

1 You are the fairest of the daughters of Eve,
   for God has chosen and blessed you.

2 Because you love justice and goodness
     and truth;
   because your heart is set on what is right.

3 So the Lord has chosen to shower you with
     gladness,
   greater than kings and queens in all their
     splendour.

4 To the one who gives ear to the word of
     the Lord
   will the Lord entrust the greatest of gifts.

5 See with what songs of gladness and rejoicing
   she is led into the palace of the King!

6 See how her beauty is loved by the King;
   yet he is her Lord, pay homage to him.

7 See how she is clothed in regal splendour
   priceless the jewels that embroider her robes.

8 May all of her children inherit her kingdom
   live with her in the courts of the Lord.

9 May this song make her name remembered
     for ever!
   May all the peoples praise her for ever
     and ever!

10 May this song make God's name remembered
      for ever!
   May all the peoples praise him for ever! Amen!

Isaiah 53:1-6

1 Who has believed what we have heard?
   To whom has God's power been revealed?
2 He grew up like a young plant in front of us,
   like a fresh sapling rises from the arid ground.
3 No beauty, no majesty,
   nothing to make us want to look at him.
4 Despised and rejected by men,
   a man of sorrows and familiar with suffering.
5 A man of sorows from whom people hid
     their faces,
   we despised him and thought he was worthless.
6 Yet ours were those sufferings he bore;
   the sorrows he carried were ours.
7 We thought God wanted him punished,
   we thought he should be struck down.
8 Yet ours were the faults for which he was
     wounded,
   crushed and brought low for our sins.
9 On him was laid the punishment that makes
     us whole,
   and by his wounds we are healed.
10 When we had wandered like sheep,
   he became the lamb that takes sins away.